Science In Your Life:

SOUND

Listen Up!

Wendy Sadler

www.raintreepublishers.co.uk
Visit our website to find out more information about **Raintree** books.

To order:
☎ Phone 44 (0) 1865 888112
📄 Send a fax to 44 (0) 1865 314091
💻 Visit the Raintree bookshop at **www.raintreepublishers.co.uk** to browse our catalogue and order online.

First published in Great Britain by Raintree,
Halley Court, Jordan Hill, Oxford OX2 8EJ,
part of Harcourt Education.
Raintree is a registered trademark
of Harcourt Education Ltd.

Editorial: Melanie Copland, Kate Buckingham,
and Lucy Beevor
Design: Victoria Bevan
and Bridge Creative Services Ltd
Picture Research: Hannah Taylor
and Catherine Bevan
Production: Duncan Gilbert

Originated by Chroma Graphics (Overseas) Pte. Ltd
Printed and bound in China by South China
Printing Company

ISBN 1 844 43661 6
10 09 08 07 06
10 9 8 7 6 5 4 3 2 1

**British Library Cataloguing in
Publication Data**
Sadler, Wendy
Sounds. – (Science in your life)
534
A full catalogue record for this book is available
from the British Library.

Acknowledgements
Alamy Images pp. 16 (Dynamic Graphics/ Photis),
15 (Lebrecht Music & Arts Photo Library), 27
(PHOTOTAKE Inc.), 10 (Robert Harding Picture
Library Ltd); Corbis pp. 4 (Gabe Palmer), 23 (Joe
McDonald), 11 (Ted Soqui); Corbis Royalty Free p. 26;
Getty Images pp. 6, 7, 9, 14, 22, 25 (PhotoDisc);
Harcourt Education Ltd pp. 8, 13, 17, 18, 20, 21t,
21m, 21b, 29 (Tudor Photography); Imagestate p. 24
(Frank Chmura); Photographers Direct p.5
(Transparencies, Inc.).

Cover photograph of sports coach blowing a whistle
reproduced with permission of Getty/Altrendo.

Contents

Any words appearing in the text in bold, **like this**, are explained in the glossary.

Sound all around you

Sound is all around you! When you close your eyes and listen hard, you can hear sounds you did not notice before. You can tell which sounds come from far away and which sounds come from near by.

When you finish reading this page, close your eyes for a few seconds and listen hard. What can you hear?

You may have made some very loud sounds today!

Think about all the different sounds you have heard today. Where did they come from? How many of the following sounds have you heard?

- alarm clock beeping to wake you up
- people speaking to you
- music on the radio
- voices coming from the television
- eggs sizzling in the frying pan
- birds singing
- traffic moving through the streets.

How many things in this kitchen make a sound?

What is sound?

Sound is a very fast wobble called a **vibration**. The vibrations move too quickly for us to see, but they can move through solid objects, liquids, and air.

Sound travels through **materials** as a wave. If you throw a stone into a pond you see ripples travelling out from where the stone hits the water. Sound waves travel in a similar way, but you cannot see them.

Sound waves are made when something vibrates. The waves spread out like ripples on a pond.

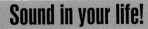

Next time there is a thunderstorm, try counting how many seconds there are between the lightning flash and the thunder bang. When there is a lot of time between them, the storm is far away. If there is not much time, then the storm is close by.

Sound travels very quickly, around 340 metres (1,115 feet) in just 1 second! But this is a lot slower than light. Sometimes in a thunderstorm you see lightning first and then hear a bang of thunder later. The thunder and lightning actually happen at the same time, but the light reaches you before the sound.

How do we make sound?

Sound **vibrations** are very fast movements backwards and forwards, or side to side. We can make sound by making something vibrate.

When you pluck a guitar string you pull it a little bit in one direction and then let go. The string wobbles from side to side very quickly. This vibration makes a sound. The wood of the guitar box also vibrates and this helps to make the sound louder.

A guitar is a string instrument. The string vibrates to make the sound.

You can also make sounds by hitting something. When you clap your hands the air is squashed up very quickly between them. This makes the air vibrate. We hear this as a sharp, sudden sound.

This is also the way that sound is made in a thunderstorm. When lightning strikes, the air around it gets hot very quickly. The air **expands** and this starts a **shockwave** that makes the rumble of thunder.

Try to clap your hands as loud as you can. How much sound can you make?

9

Echoes

Sound waves can bounce off hard **surfaces** and travel back to where they came from! This is called an **echo**. In a big room or large cave there can be quite a long time between hearing the sound you make and then hearing the echo come back to you. This is because the sound has further to travel so it takes longer. This is why echoes are best in big places.

A clap is a good sound to make echoes within a cave.

If something **reflects** sound, the sound bounces off. If something **absorbs** sound, it takes the sound in. Hard, shiny surfaces are good at reflecting sounds and making echoes. Dull, soft surfaces are good at absorbing sounds and they do not make echoes.

In bathrooms there are usually lots of hard, shiny tiles on the wall. They reflect a lot of sound. This means that your voice sounds louder when you are singing in the bath!

Concert halls have lots of shiny surfaces to help reflect the sounds of the orchestra.

Sound in your life!

Try singing in a room that has curtains, carpets, and other soft things in it. What is the sound like? Now try singing in the bathroom. Does it sound different?

What is music?

To make music you need to put different sounds together in the right way. Music needs to have a mix of different **notes** so that it is interesting to listen to. High notes are sounds that have fast **vibrations**. They have a high **pitch**. Low notes are ones that have slow vibrations. They have a low pitch.

The **volume** of a sound is how loud it is. Music has to have sounds that are different volumes. Loud sounds have lots of **energy** and quiet sounds have less energy.

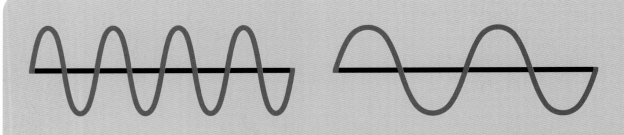

Fast vibrations = high pitch   Slow vibrations = low pitch

When there are lots of waves close together we get a high pitch. When the waves spread out we get a low pitch.

Music also has something called **rhythm**. This means that long and short notes are put together to make patterns in the music. The rhythm is the part of the music that you can tap your feet to, or dance to.

Sound in your life!

Put your hand on your chest and feel your heartbeat. Your heartbeat has its own rhythm. When you are running around it has a fast rhythm. When you are resting or sleeping it has a slow rhythm.

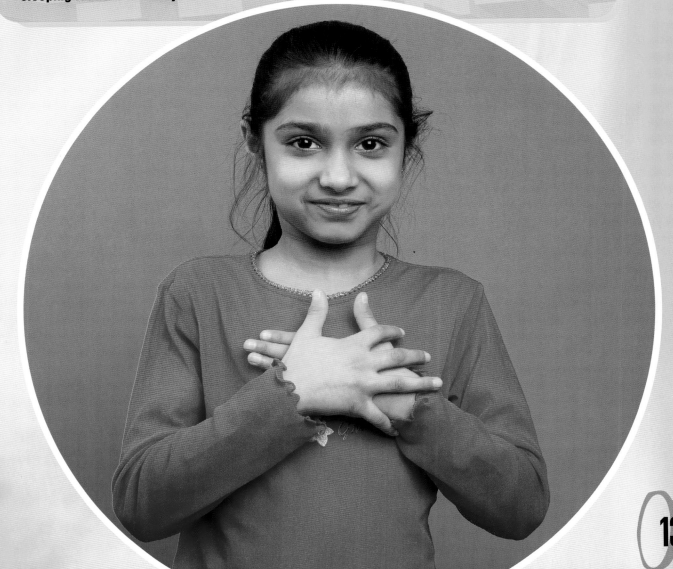

Making music

To make music, first of all we need to make something **vibrate**. Different musical instruments make vibrations in different ways.

String instruments, such as guitars and violins, use the vibrations of the strings to make music. A violin is played using a bow made of lots of fine hair. As the bow rubs across the strings it sticks to the string, then slips away again very quickly. This sticking and slipping makes the strings vibrate.

A violin has strings that can be plucked with the fingers or played with a bow.

Wind instruments, such as recorders or flutes, use vibrating air to make sounds. **Percussion** instruments, such as drums or cymbals, have to be hit to make a sound.

A piano could be called a percussion instrument or a string instrument! Inside the piano are tiny hammers and a lot of strings. When you press a key the hammer hits the string inside to make the sound.

strings

Inside a piano there are lots of strings that get hit by small hammers to make sounds.

Recording sound

When you listen to music on a CD you are hearing a recording of the singer or the group. When you make a recording, you use a microphone to turn the sound waves into an electric wave. The electric wave can be saved and played back later when you want to enjoy your music.

You can carry recorded music with you wherever you go!

What would happen without CDs?

If we did not have music recordings or CDs we could only listen to music when it is played live. A music recording lets you listen to your favourite music any time and almost anywhere.

A CD can store music as a pattern of numbers.

Most people now listen to music on CD or **MP3**. This is called **digital** recording. To make a digital recording you have to turn the pattern of sound waves into numbers. Inside your CD player a **laser beam** reads these numbers as a **code**. The code is then turned back into a sound wave so you can enjoy your favourite tunes!

How do we hear?

We use our ears to hear sound. The flaps of skin on the sides of your head are shaped so that they can catch sounds as they come through the air.

Sound in your life!

Try making cup shapes with your hands and putting them around your ears. This makes a larger flap to catch sounds. What happens to the sounds you hear?

After your ears catch sound it travels down the hole in your ear. It hits a thin piece of skin called the eardrum. The eardrum **vibrates** and this vibration is passed on to some tiny bones inside your ear.

Right down inside your ear there are some special hairs. These pick up the movements of the tiny bones and turn them into an electrical **signal**. This signal goes to your brain to tell you that you have heard a sound.

If you listen to lots of loud sounds these hairs can get damaged. If the hairs stop working you cannot hear very well.

Your ear collects sound. The vibrations are turned into messages in your brain.

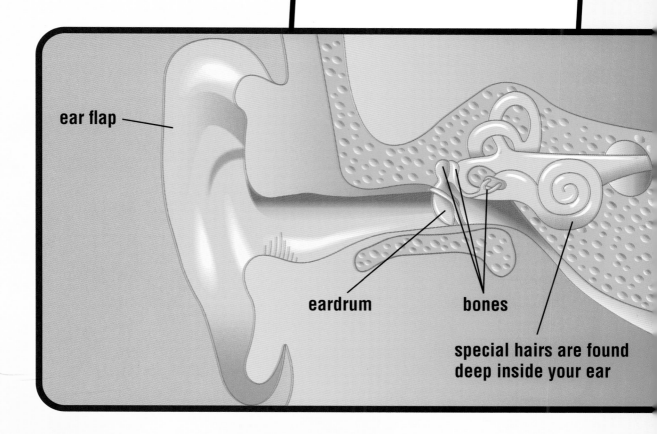

ear flap

eardrum

bones

special hairs are found deep inside your ear

How do we speak?

Inside your throat there are folds of skin called **vocal chords**. When you speak you push air from your **lungs** through these. As the air moves through the vocal chords it makes them **vibrate**. These vibrations make the sound of your voice.

Sound in your life!

Blow up a balloon and hold it by the neck. Now stretch the neck of the balloon out so the air has to push between the bits of rubber in the neck of the balloon. Can you make a sound? This is what you are doing inside your throat when you speak!

The air coming out makes the rubber of the balloon vibrate. This makes a loud squeaking noise!

You use your teeth, lips, and mouth to make different sounds with the vibrations. Say "aahh", "oooo", and "eeee" with your fingers touching your lips. Can you feel the different shapes you make?

Try making different sounds with your teeth, lips, and mouth.

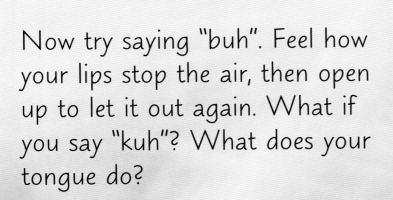

Now try saying "buh". Feel how your lips stop the air, then open up to let it out again. What if you say "kuh"? What does your tongue do?

21

Animals and sounds

Animals do not talk, but they can use sounds to send messages. They can send messages to tell another animal about danger, or to scare off an animal that might hurt them.

Cats sometimes hiss at other cats to scare them off. A dog might bark if it wants to go for a walk, or if it hears a strange noise. Even animals in the sea make sounds. Whales make musical sounds that can travel very far to reach other whales in the sea.

This frog makes very loud sounds using the pouch of skin under its throat.

This bat can use sound and echoes to find things to eat in the dark.

Animals can hear some sounds that humans cannot hear. A dog can hear very high-pitched sounds that we cannot hear. Some dogs are trained using dog whistles. We cannot hear the whistle sounds, but they are very loud to the dog.

Other animals use sounds and **echoes** to find their way around when they cannot see. Bats send out high-pitched sounds then pick up the echo as it bounces off things. This tells them where things are. They can even find tiny insects to eat by picking up these echoes.

Danger!

Sound is very useful as a warning because you can hear it wherever it is coming from. When light is used as a warning it can sometimes get blocked if something is in the way. This does not happen with sound.

When you are crossing the road there is sometimes a green light and a sound that helps you know when it is safe to cross. You should always look and listen before you start crossing!

Sound in your life!

How many different kinds of warning sounds can you think of?

Sound and light help us to cross the road safely.

A smoke alarm makes a noise if it **detects** smoke. This can save your life because the sound wakes you up if you are asleep.

Sometimes people need to get through traffic very quickly when they are on their way to help someone. Fire engines, police cars, and ambulances have loud sirens so that people can move their cars out of the way and let them through.

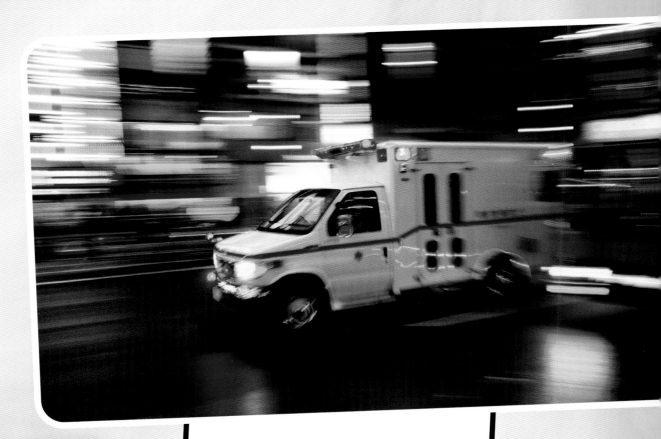

Sound can be used to help clear the way for ambulances.

Sounds in your body

Our bodies make lots of noises. Some sounds are made as your food passes through your body. When food reaches your stomach, very strong **chemicals** break the food down into a slushy mixture. This can make bubbling noises after you have eaten. When the food gets further along it can make gas. This gas can make you burp because your body wants to get rid of the gas.

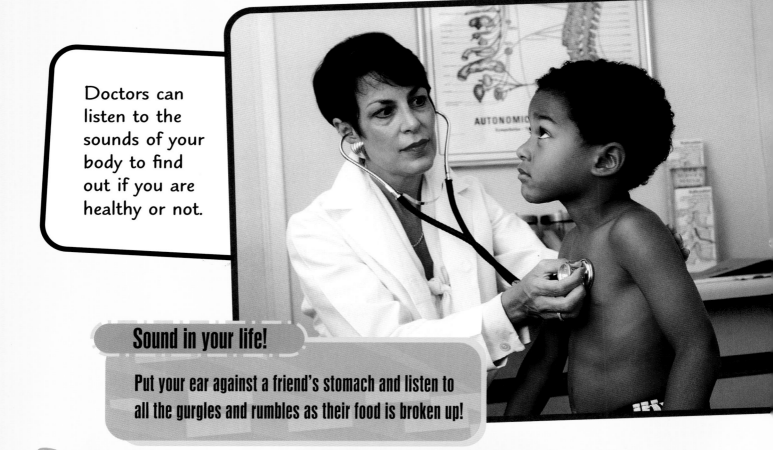

Doctors can listen to the sounds of your body to find out if you are healthy or not.

Sound in your life!

Put your ear against a friend's stomach and listen to all the gurgles and rumbles as their food is broken up!

Other moving parts in your body also make sounds. If you are very quiet, you can even hear your heart beating!

Some machines make a very high-pitched sound that we cannot hear. This is called **ultrasound**. By sending ultrasounds into the body and measuring the **echoes**, doctors can make a picture of what is inside. These machines are used to look at babies inside their mothers before they are born!

This machine uses sound and echoes to make a picture of the baby inside this mother's body.

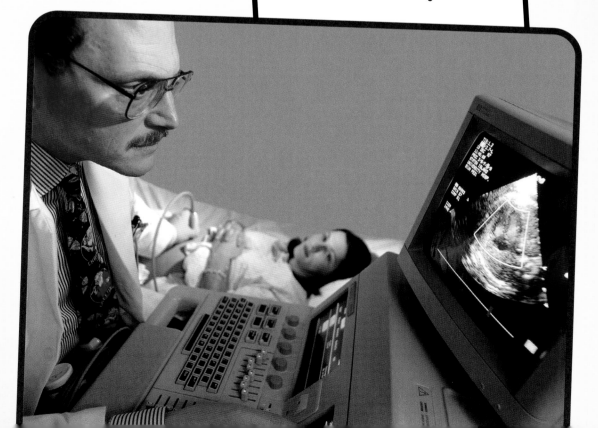

Facts about sound

Humans can hear a range of sounds from 20 **vibrations** per second up to 20,000 vibrations per second.

Sounds that are faster than 20,000 vibrations per second are called **ultrasound**. Sounds that are slower than 20 vibrations per second are called infrasound.

Elephants can hear very slow vibrations of just 4 per second!

The **volume** or loudness of sound is measured in decibels (dB). Here are some examples of different sounds and how loud they are:

- ticking of a watch 20 dB
- alarm clock 80 dB
- lawn mower 95 dB
- jet aeroplane engine 130 dB.

Did you know?

- Sound travels slightly slower on cold days or at high places!
- Your throat makes different shapes to make different sounds.
- Some aeroplanes can fly faster than the speed of sound.
- A sperm whale makes the loudest sound of any animal on Earth.

Find out more

You can find out more about science in everyday life by talking to your teacher or parents. Your local library will also have books that can help. You will find the answers to many of your questions in this book. If you want to know more, you can use other books and the Internet.

Books to read

Discovering Science: Sound, Rebecca Hunter
   (Raintree, 2003)
Science Answers: Sound, Chris Cooper
   (Heinemann Library, 2003)
Science Files: Sound, Steve Parker
   (Heinemann Library, 2004)

Using the Internet

Explore the Internet to find out more about sound. Try using a search engine such as www.yahooligans.com or www.internet4kids.com, and type in keywords such as **"percussion"**, **"pitch"**, and **"ultrasound"**.

Glossary

absorb take in. Sound can be absorbed by some objects.

chemical special substance. Everything around us is made of chemicals. Some are natural and some are man-made.

code way of sending messages using numbers, letters, or shapes

detect read or pick up a signal or message

digital when sound is stored as numbers

echo sound that bounces off a surface and comes back to your ears

energy power to make things work. You need energy to get up and walk or run around.

expand get bigger

laser beam powerful light of just one colour with a very narrow beam

lungs part of your body inside your chest that you breathe air into

material something that objects are made from

MP3 type of computer file that stores music

notes musical sounds that have different numbers of vibrations in a second, notes can be put together to make music

percussion when a sound is made by hitting something. A drum is a percussion instrument.

pitch speed of vibrations in a sound. High-pitched sounds have fast vibrations, low pitched sounds have slow vibrations.

reflect bounce off

rhythm repeated pattern of sounds or movements

shockwave sudden movement of air

signal sign or message

surface top or outside part of an object

ultrasound sound that is higher than humans can hear

vibrate move up and down or backwards and forwards very quickly

vocal chord thin pieces of skin inside your throat that vibrate when you speak

volume how loud or quiet a sound is

31

Index

Titles in the *Science In Your Life* series include:

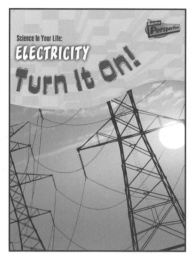

Hardback   1 184 443658 6

Hardback   1 844 43662 4

Hardback   1 844 43659 4

Hardback   1 844 43663 2

Hardback   1 844 43660 8

Hardback   1 844 43664 0

Hardback   1 844 43661 6

Find out about the other titles in this series on our website www.raintreepublishers.co.uk